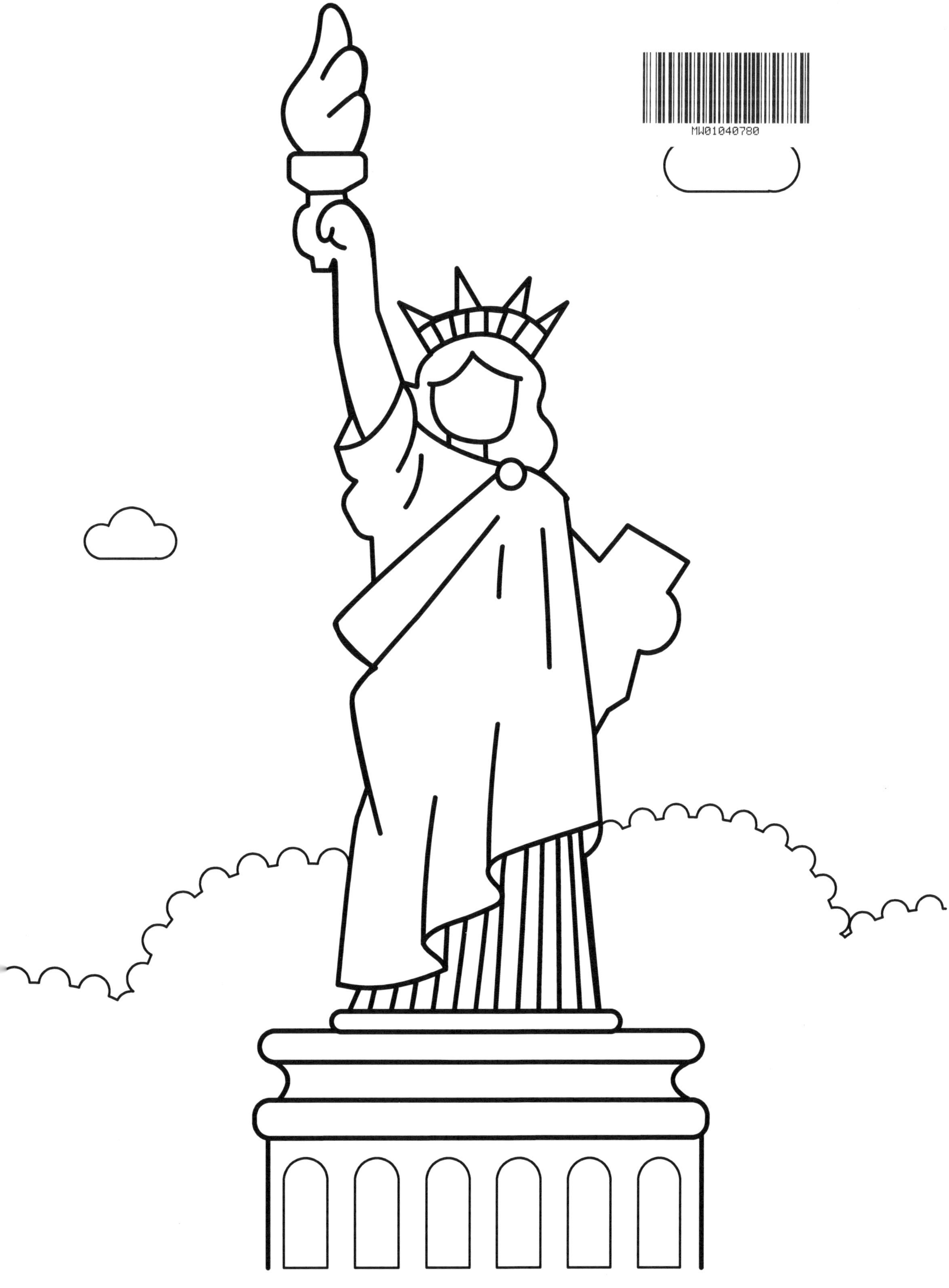

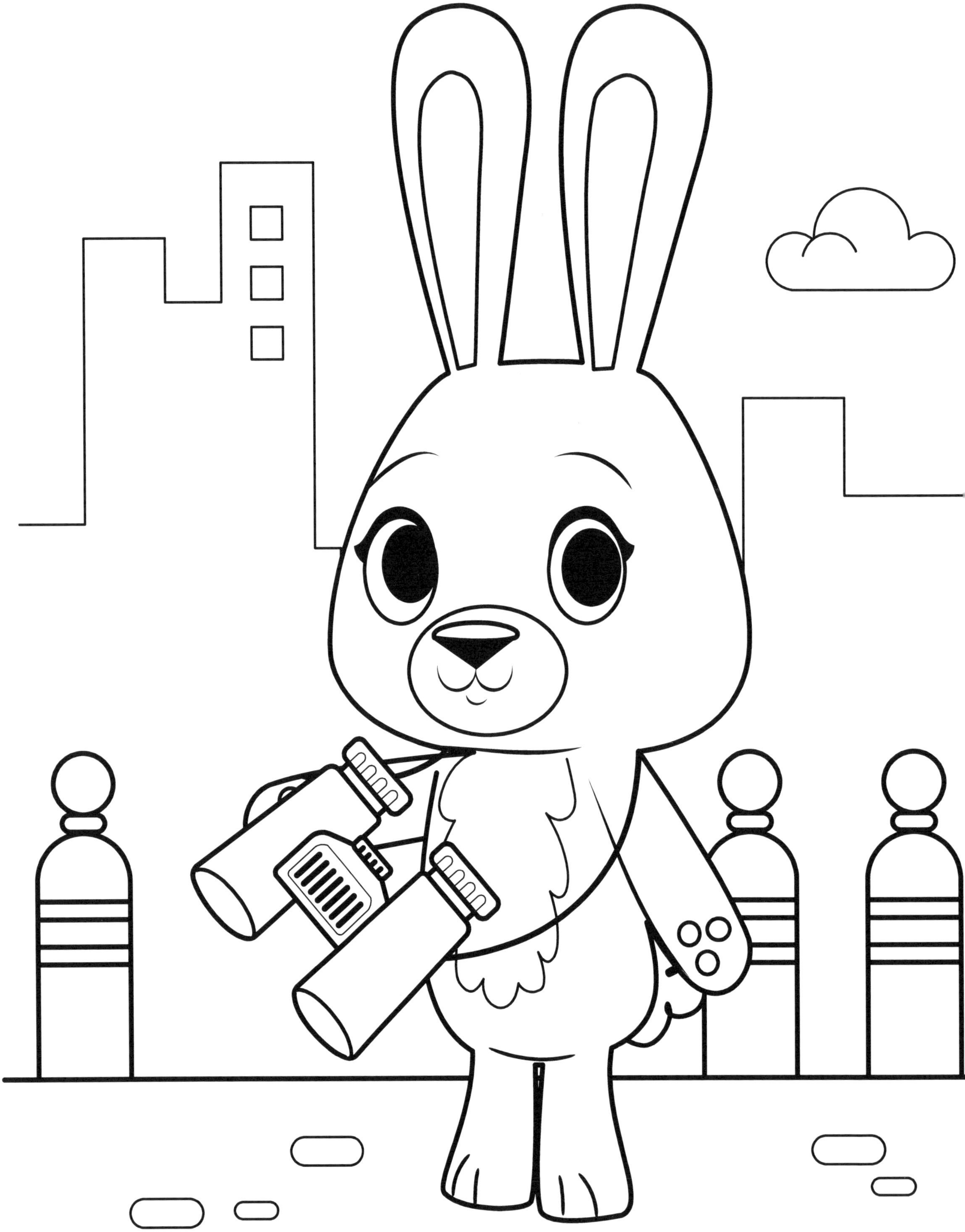

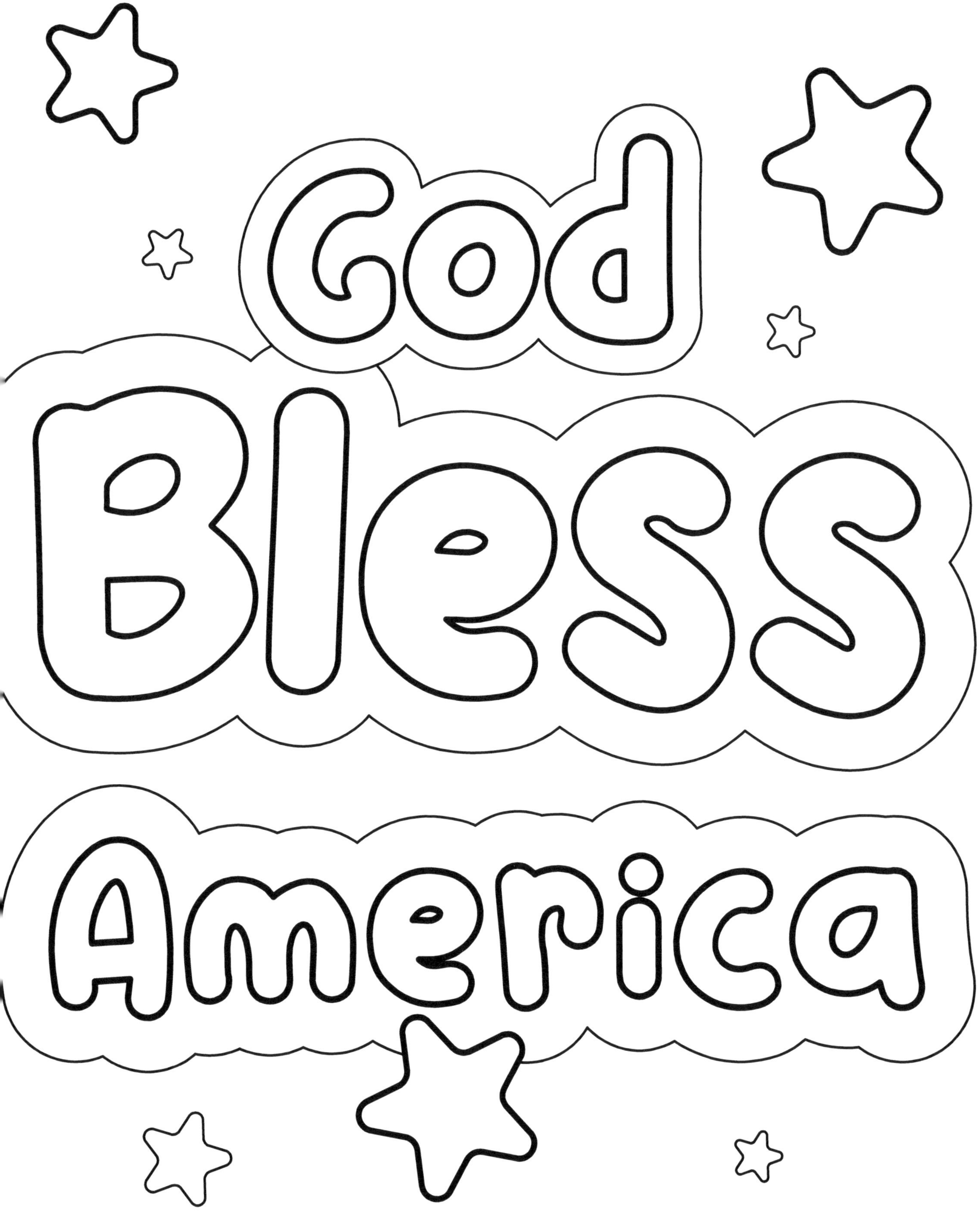
God
Bless
America

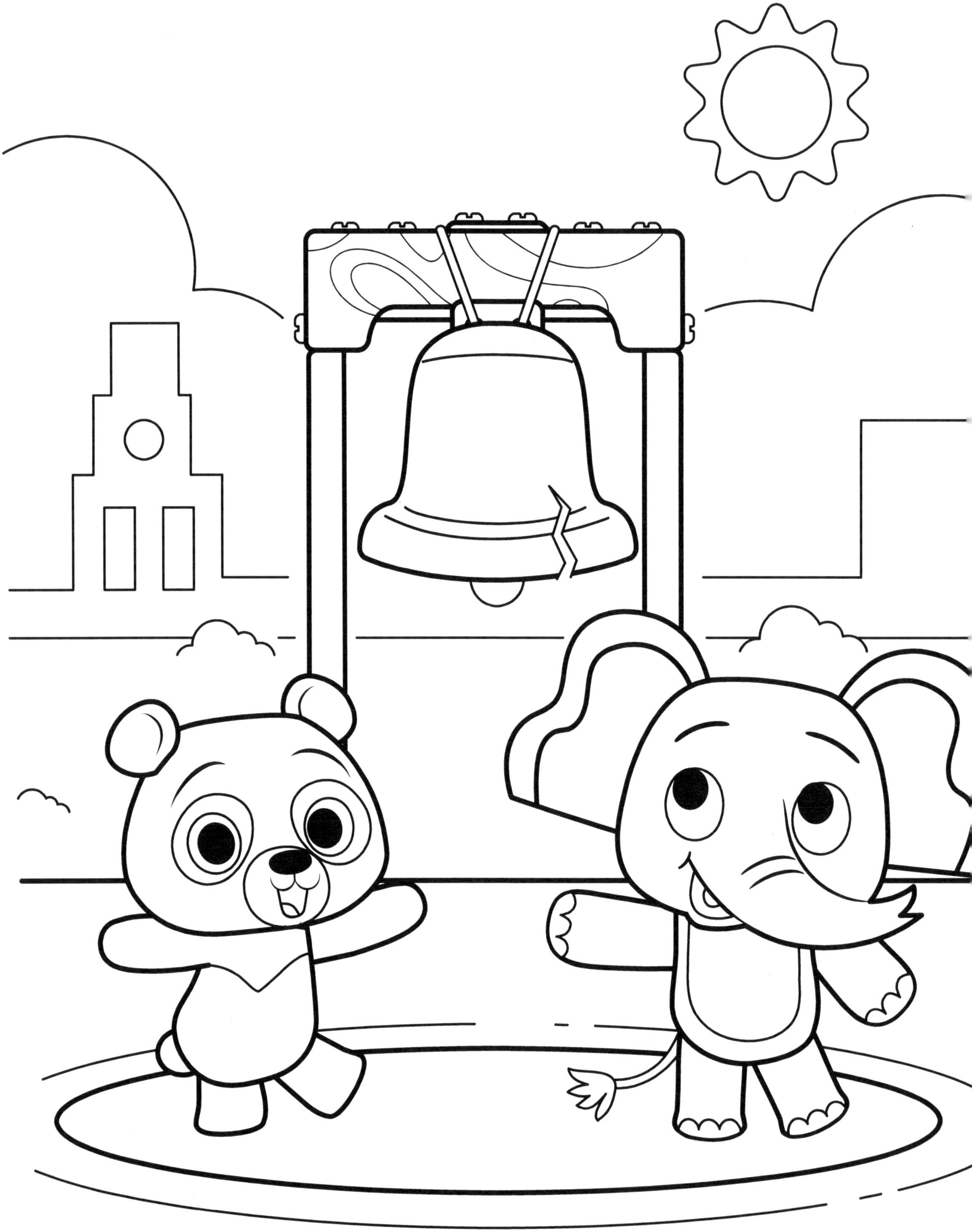

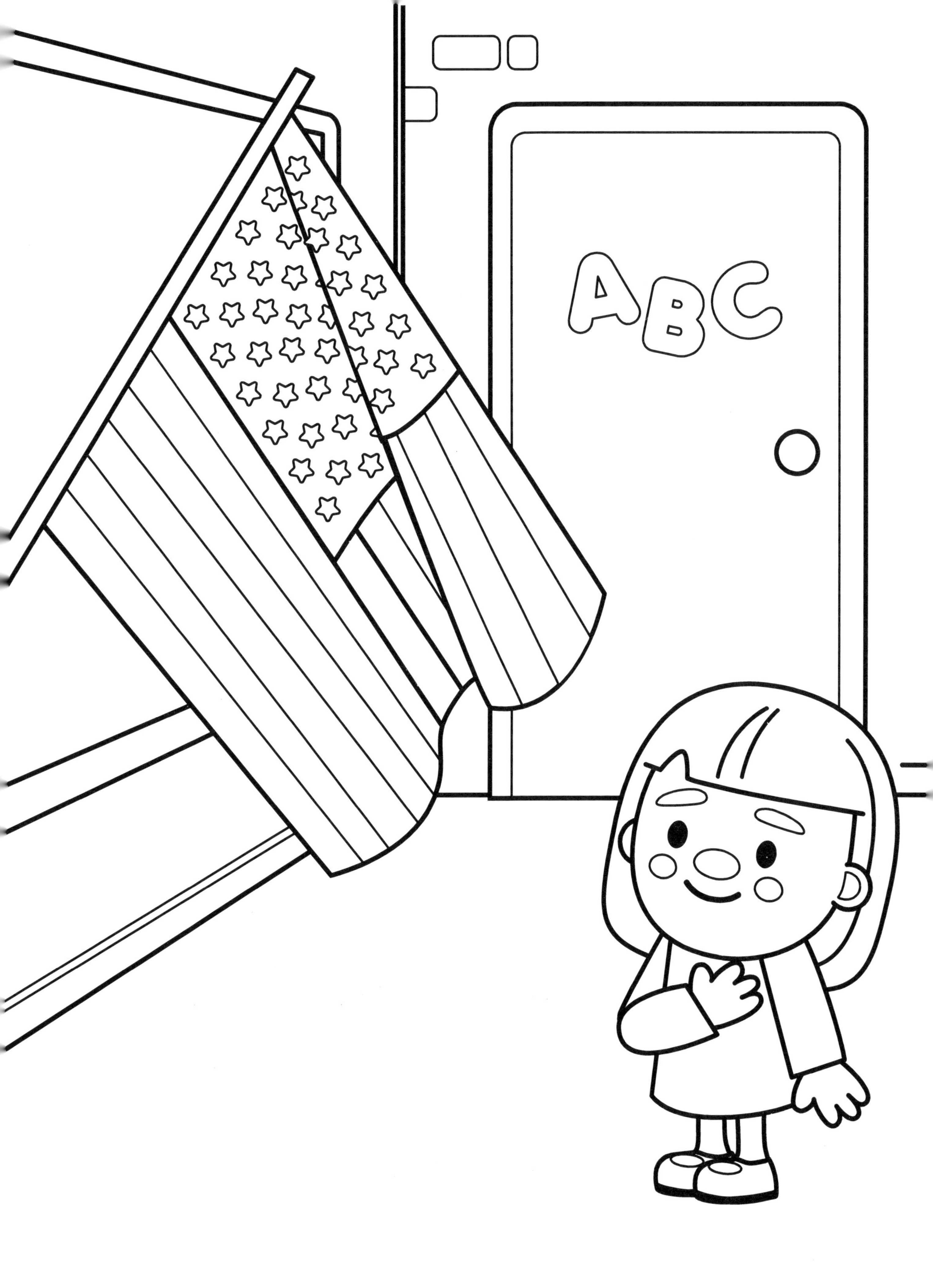
ABC

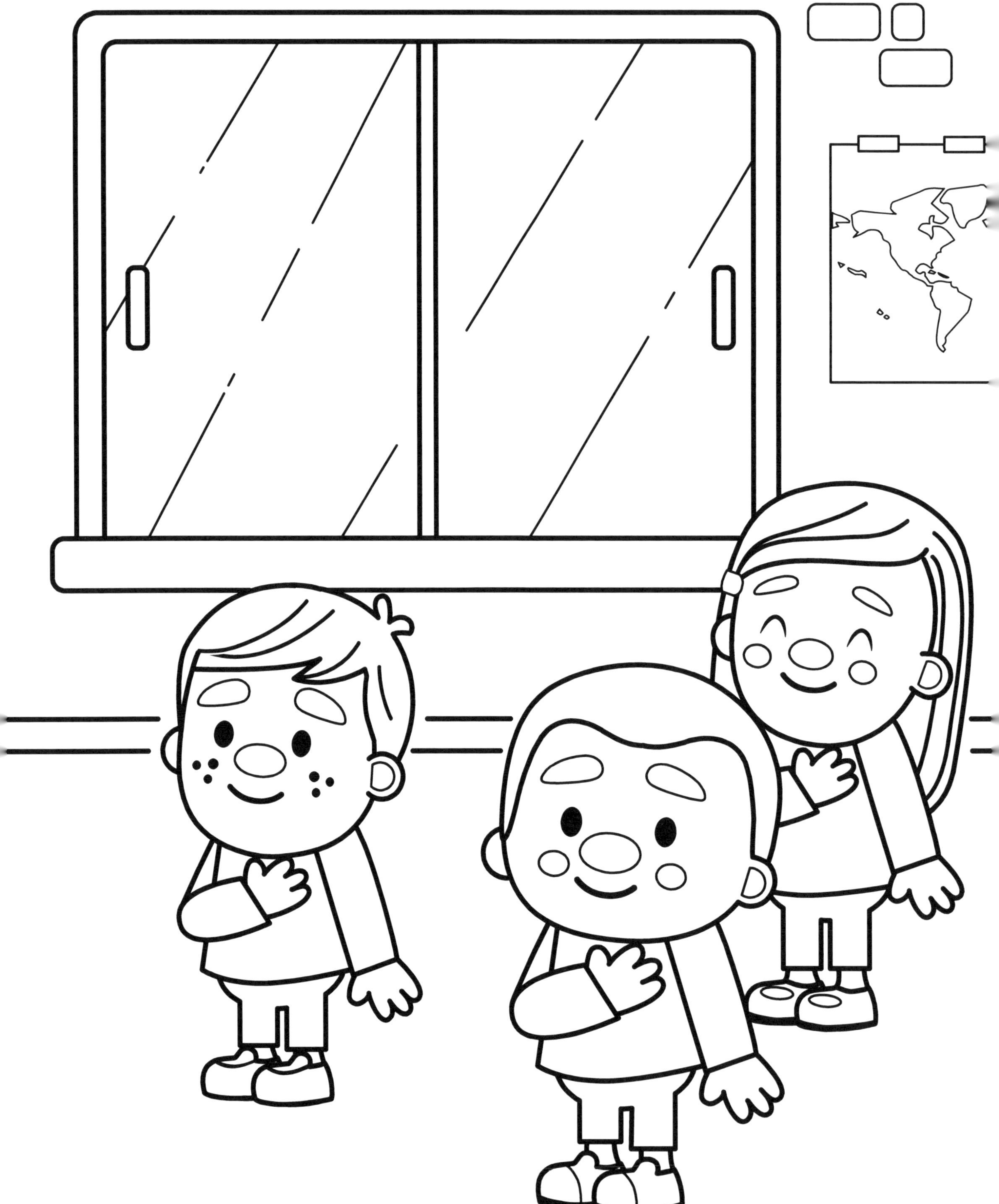

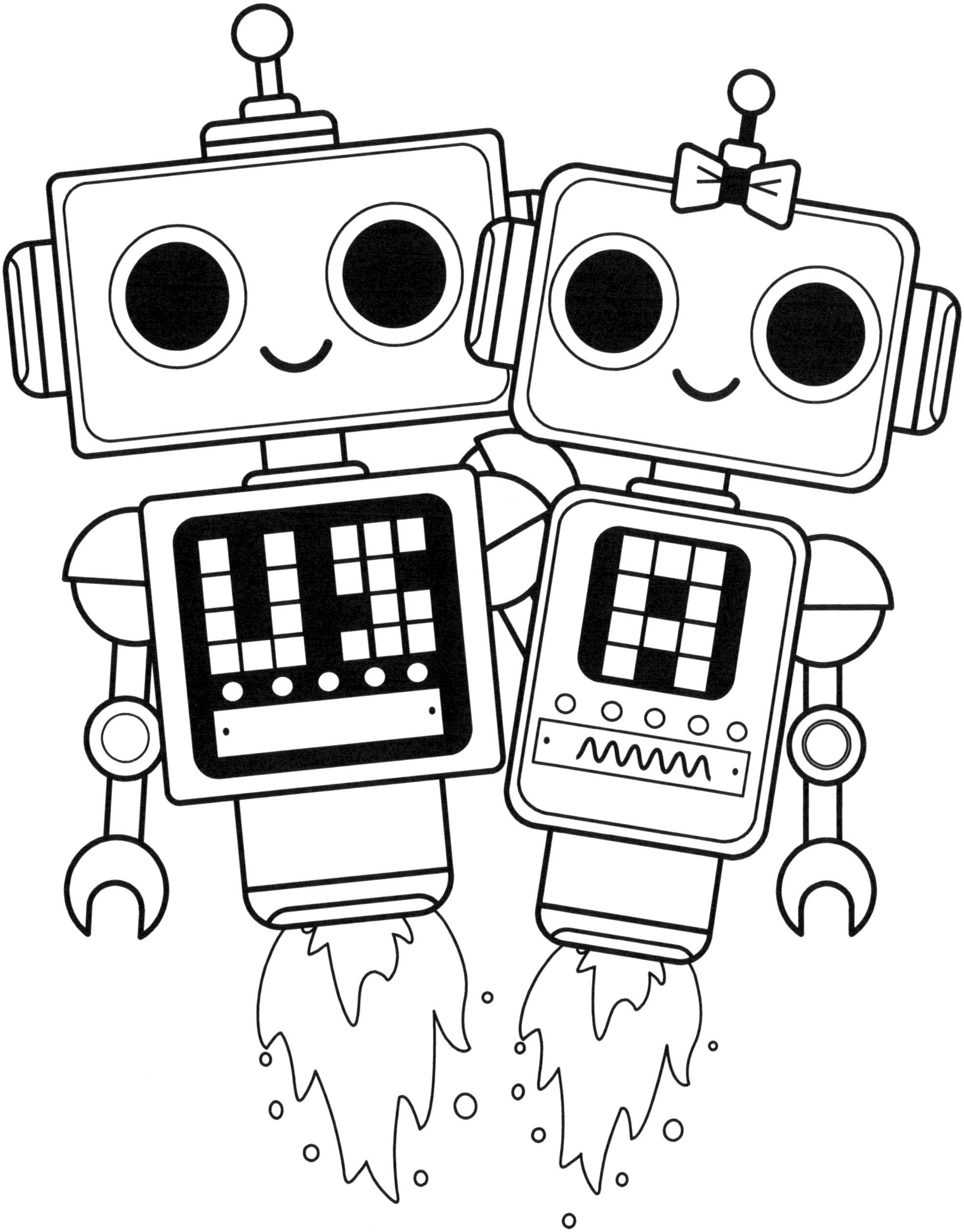

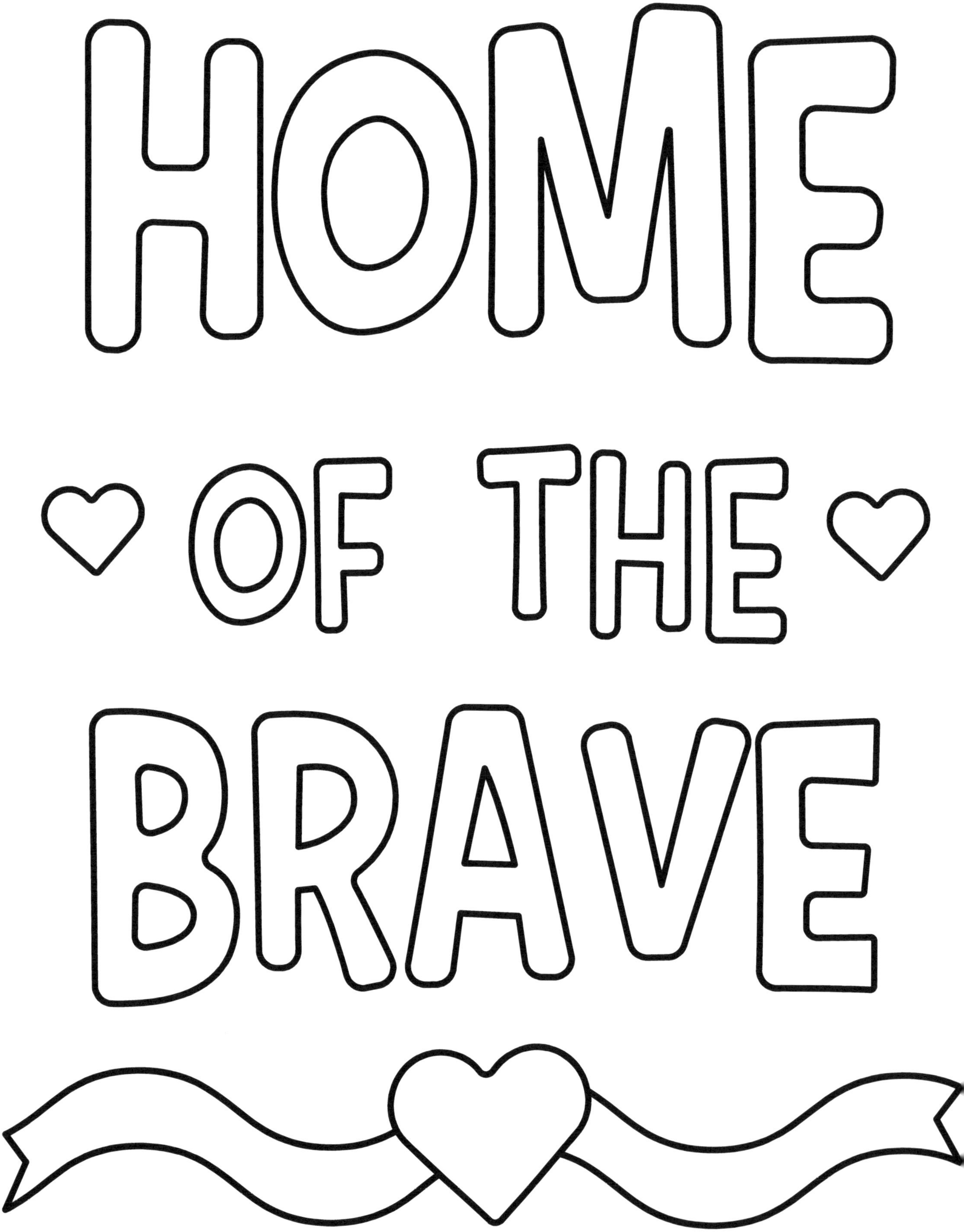
HOME
OF THE
BRAVE

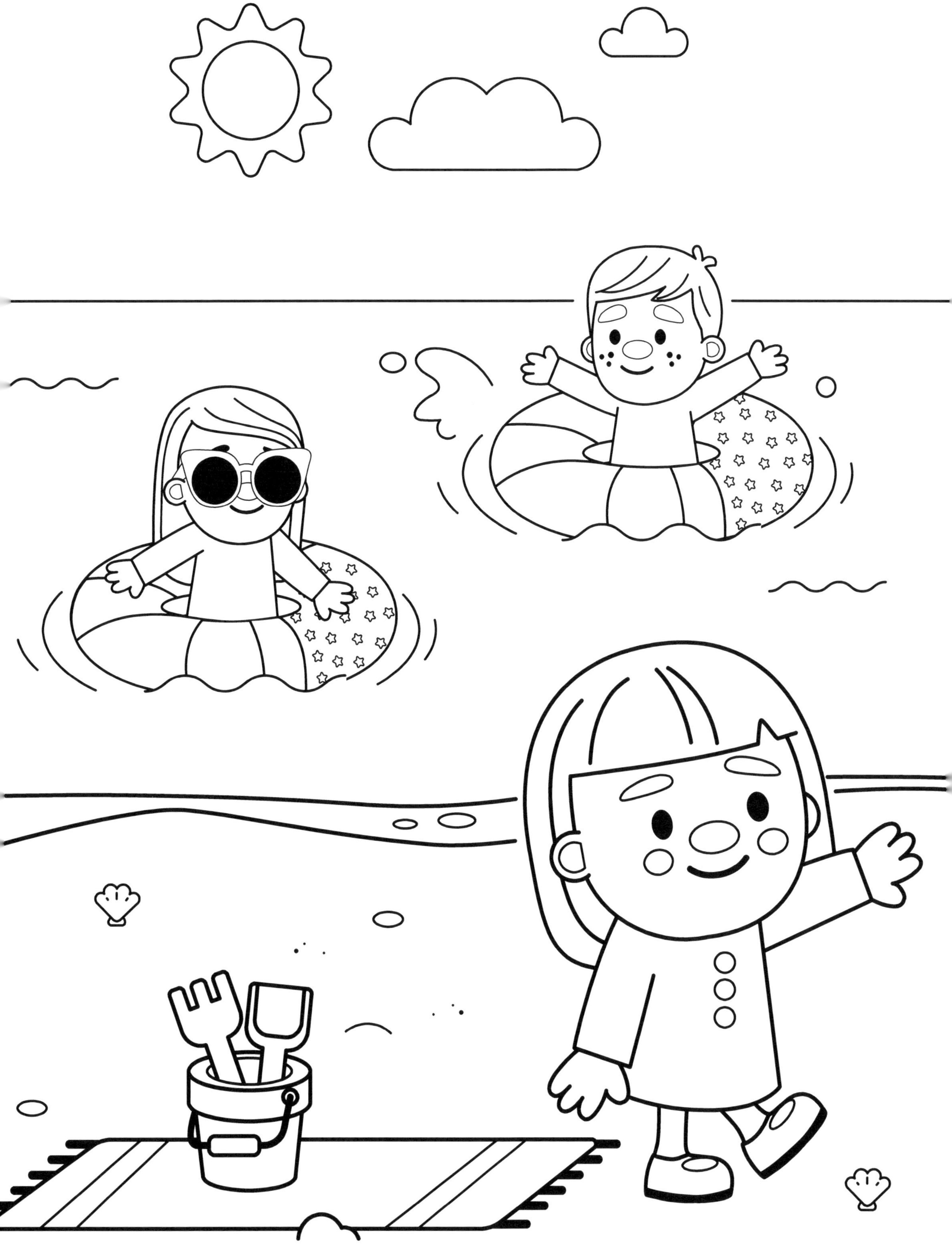

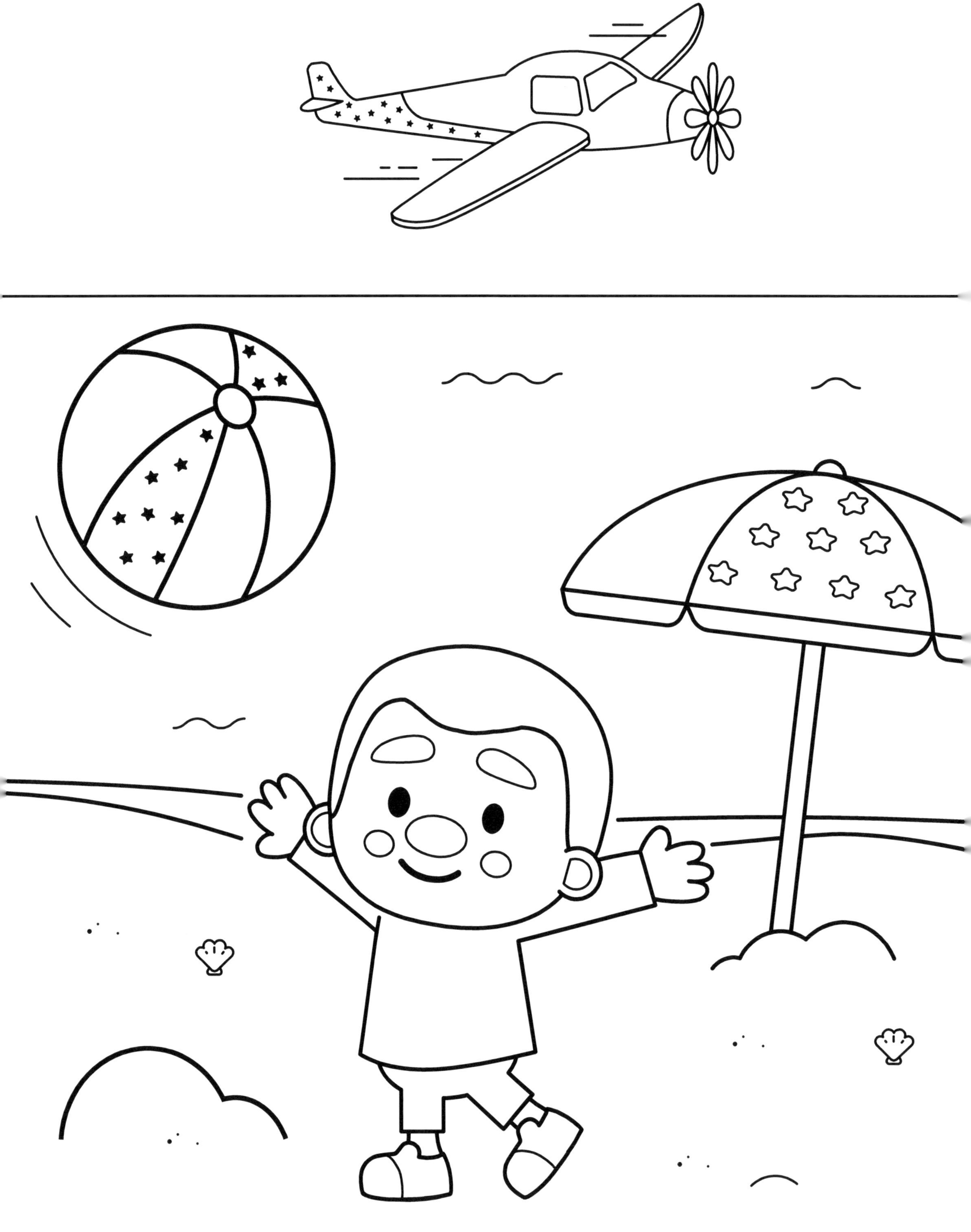

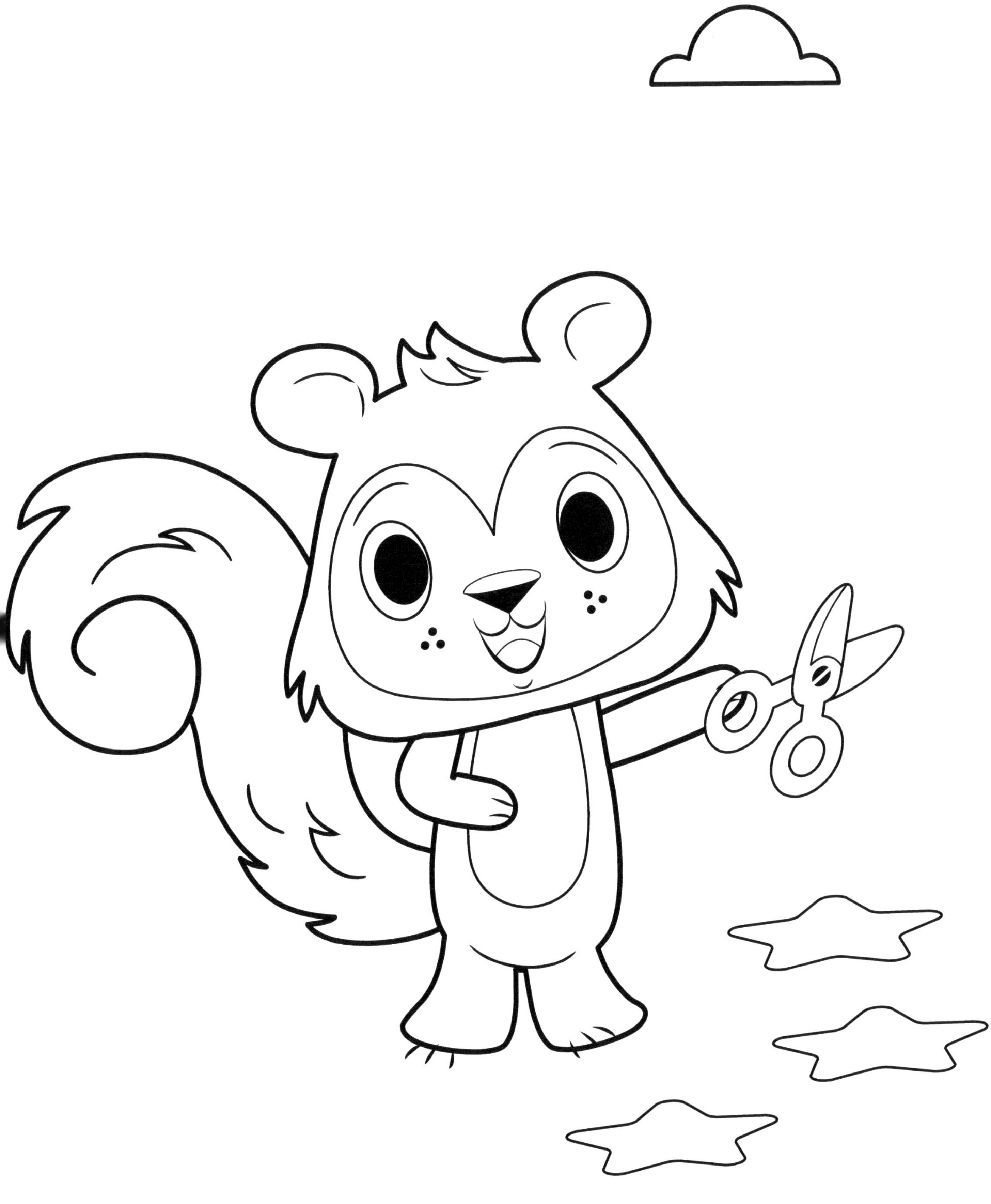

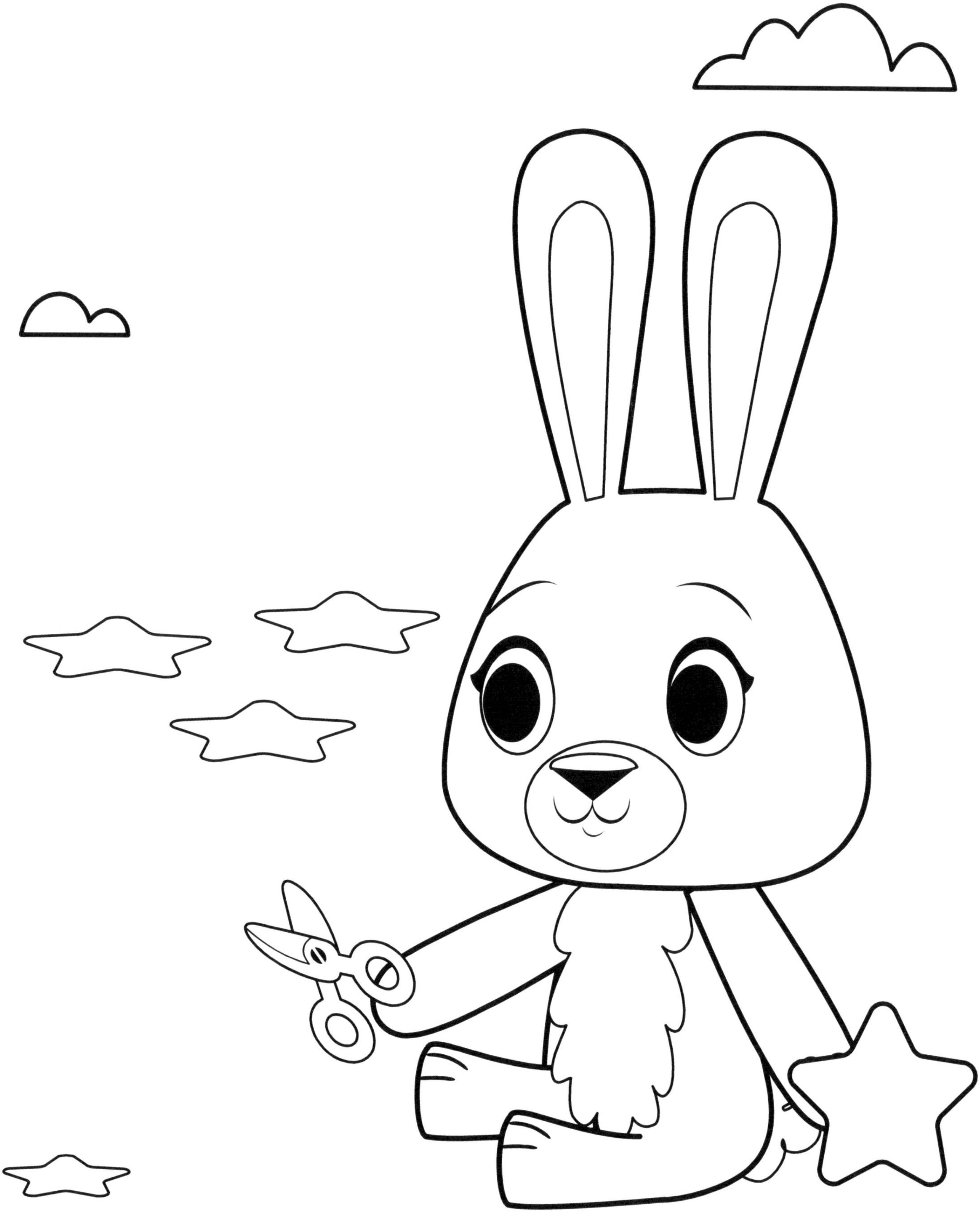

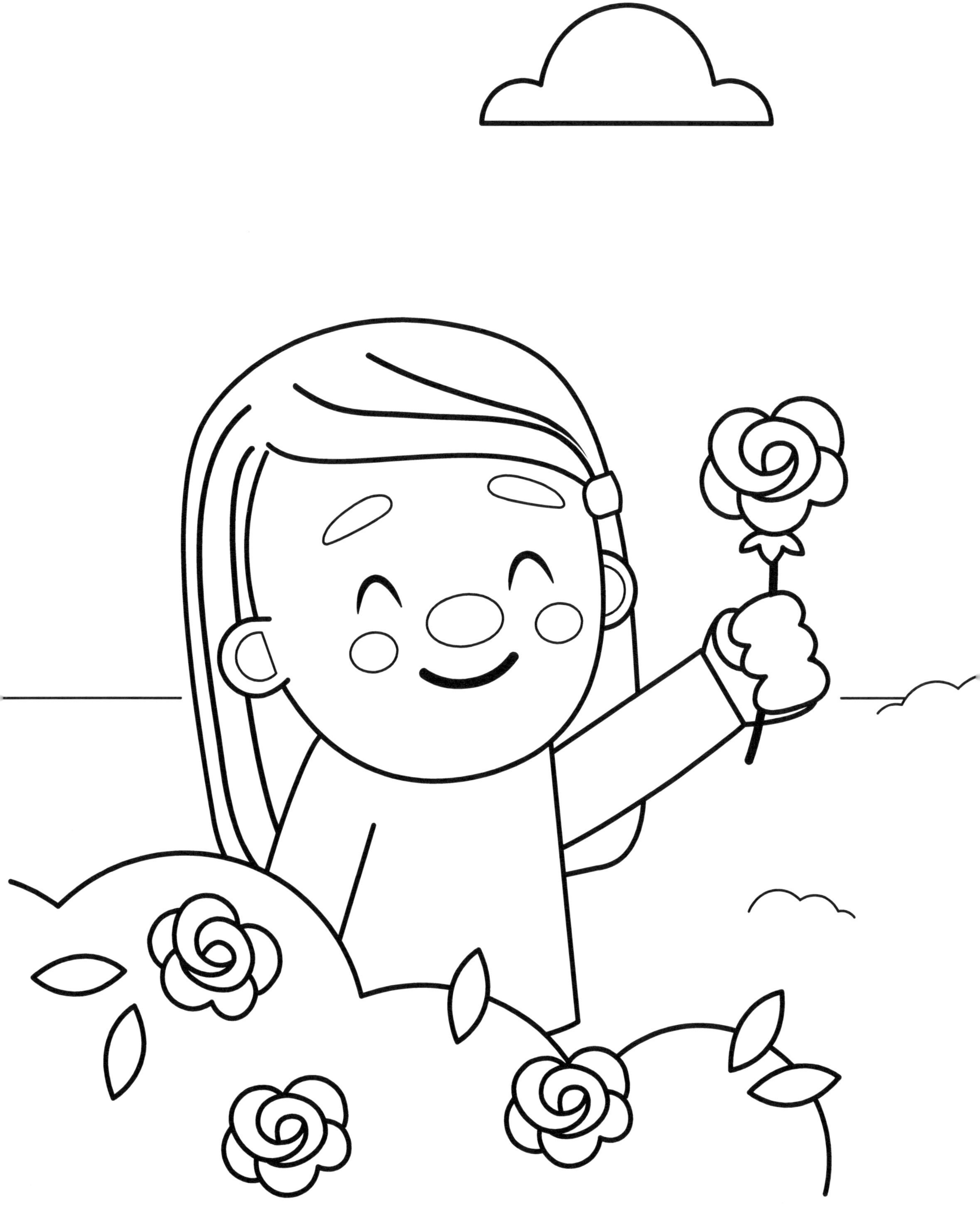

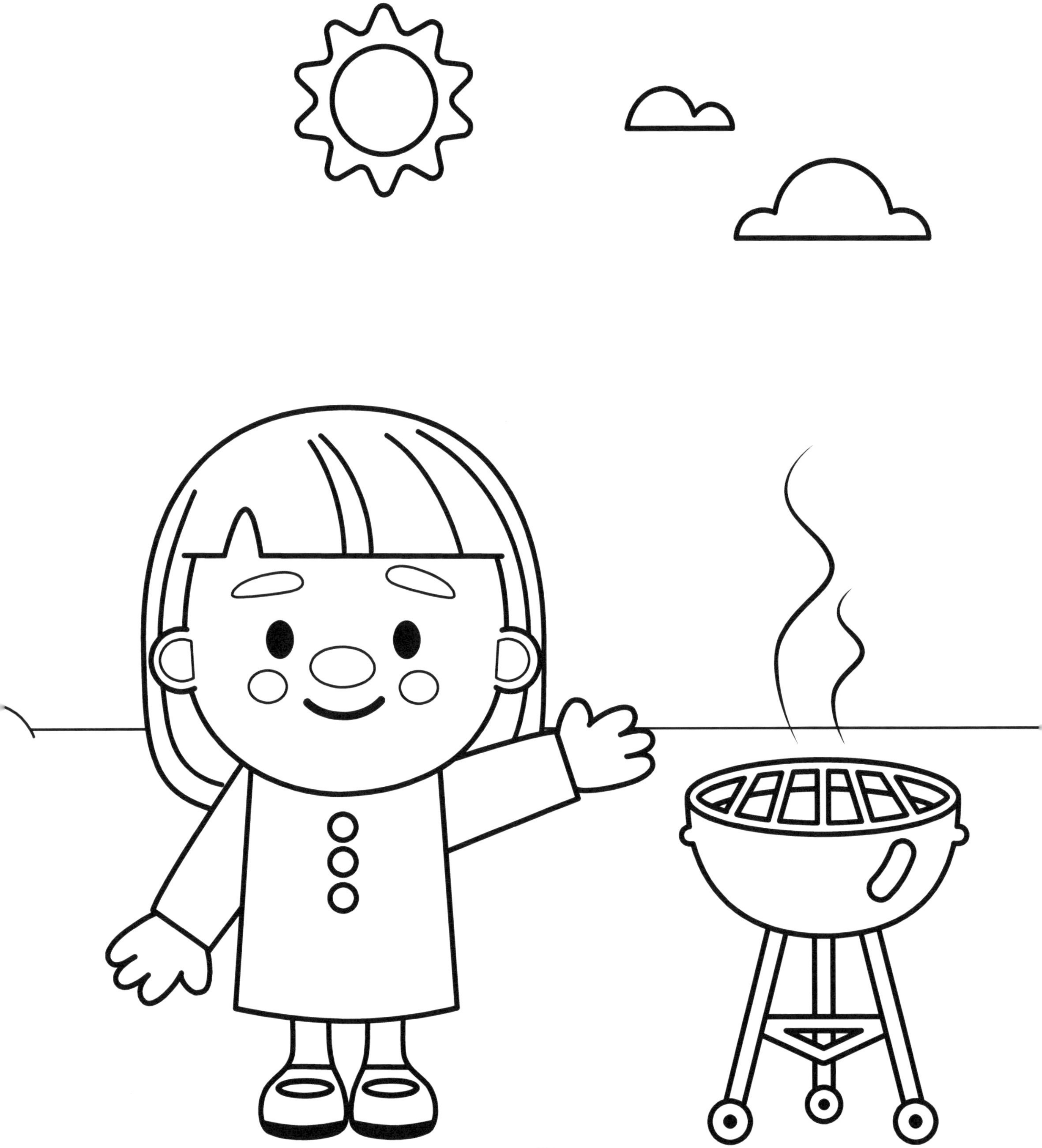

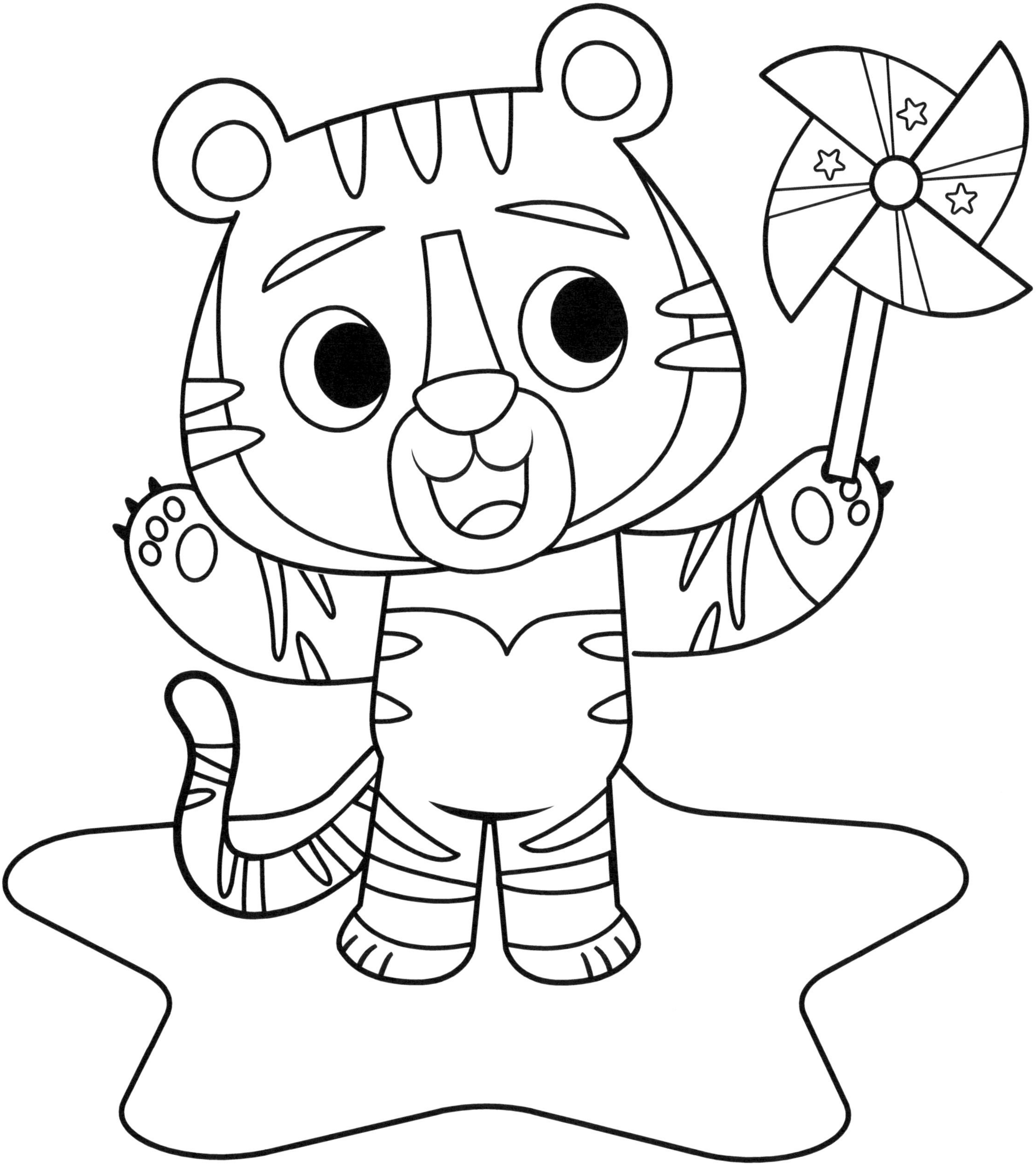

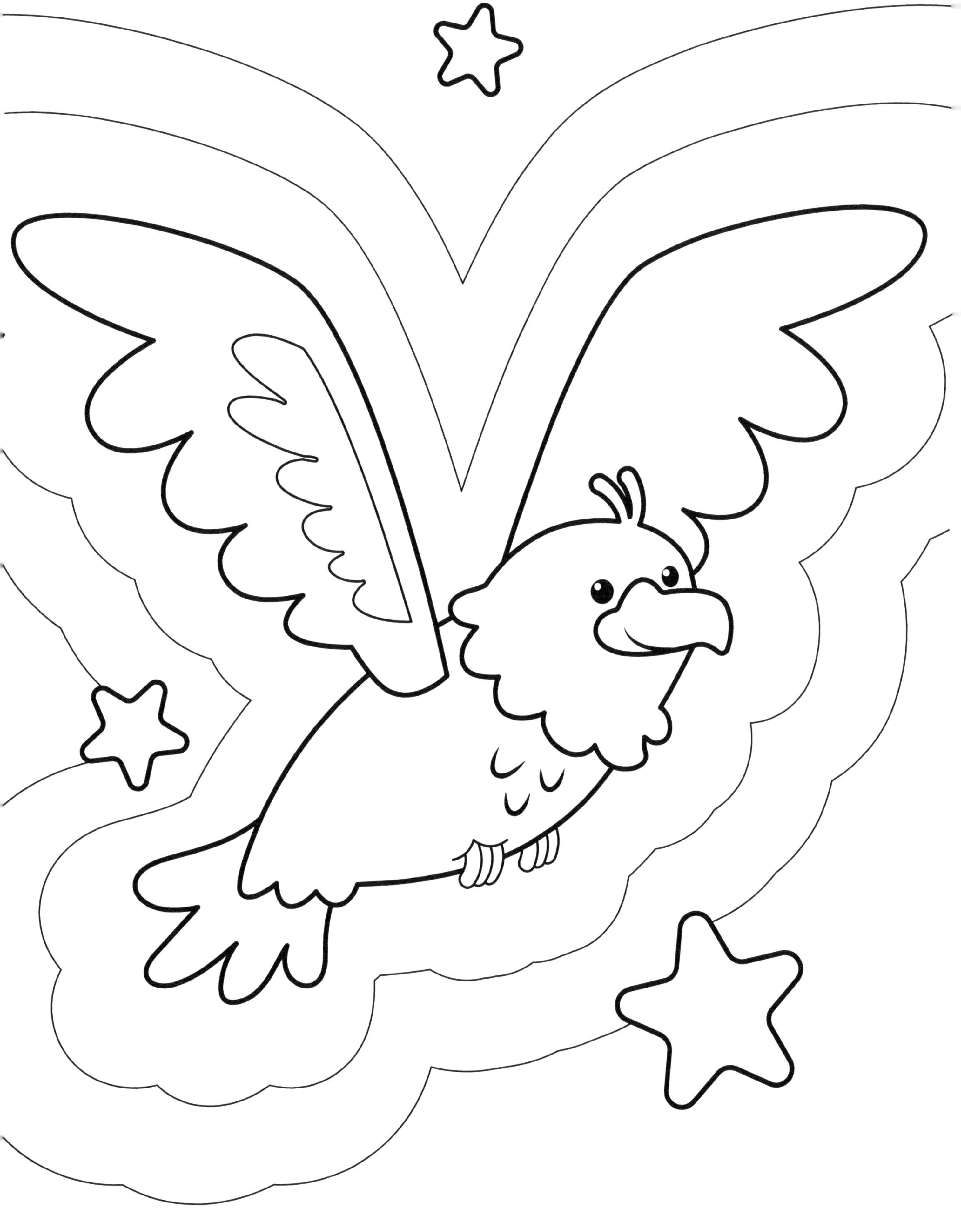

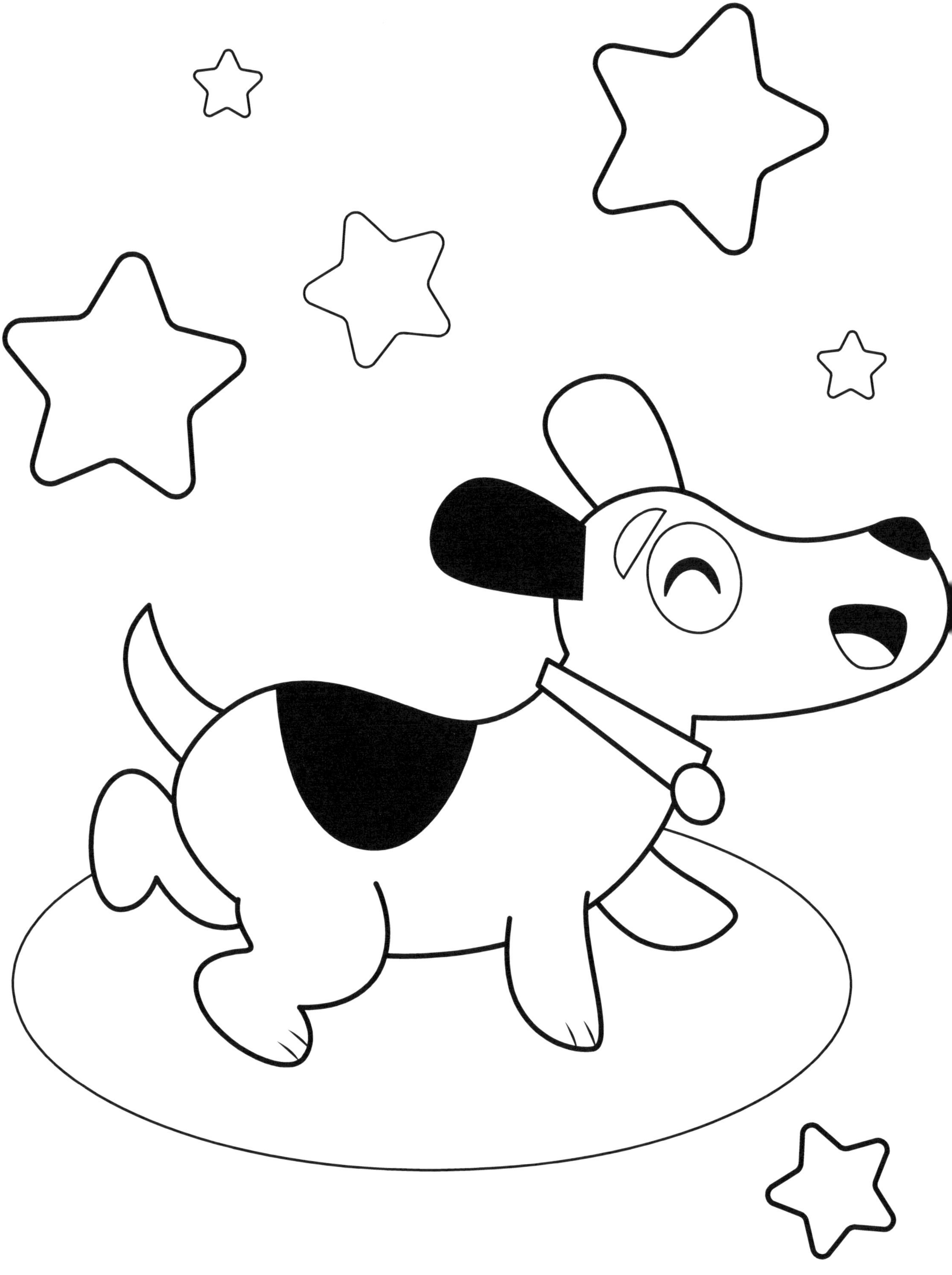

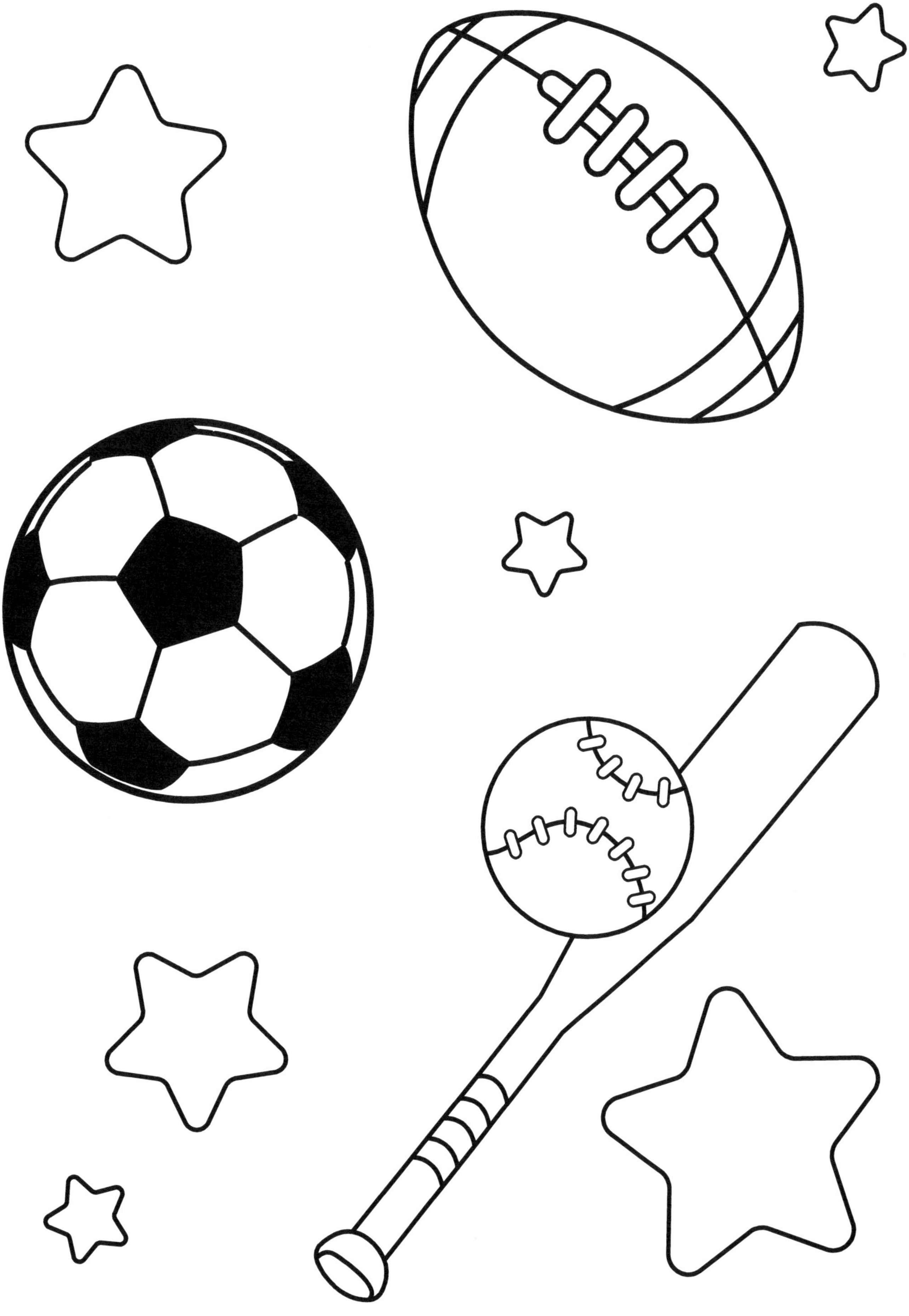

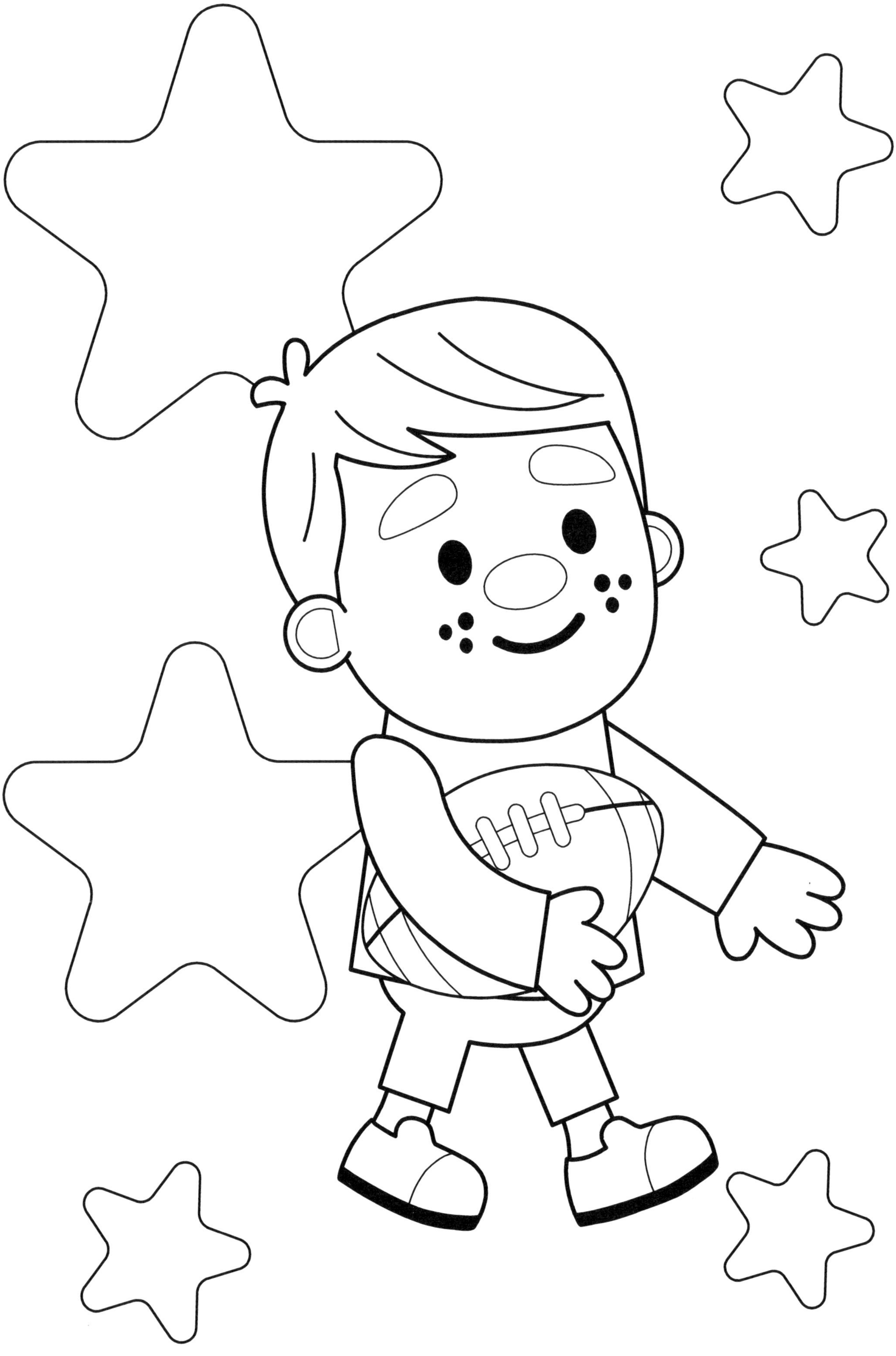

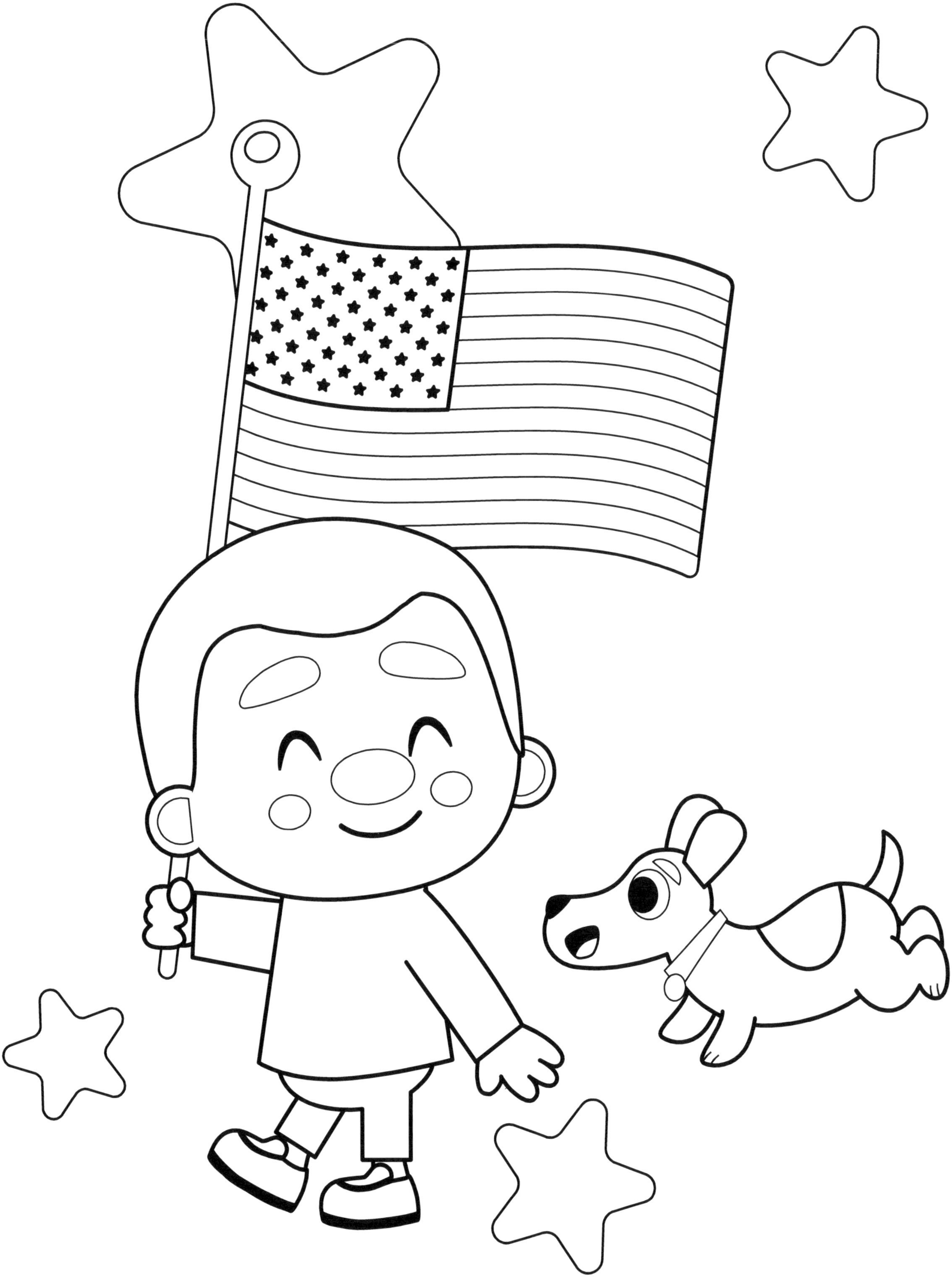

BLESSED IS THE NATION WHOSE GOD IS THE LORD

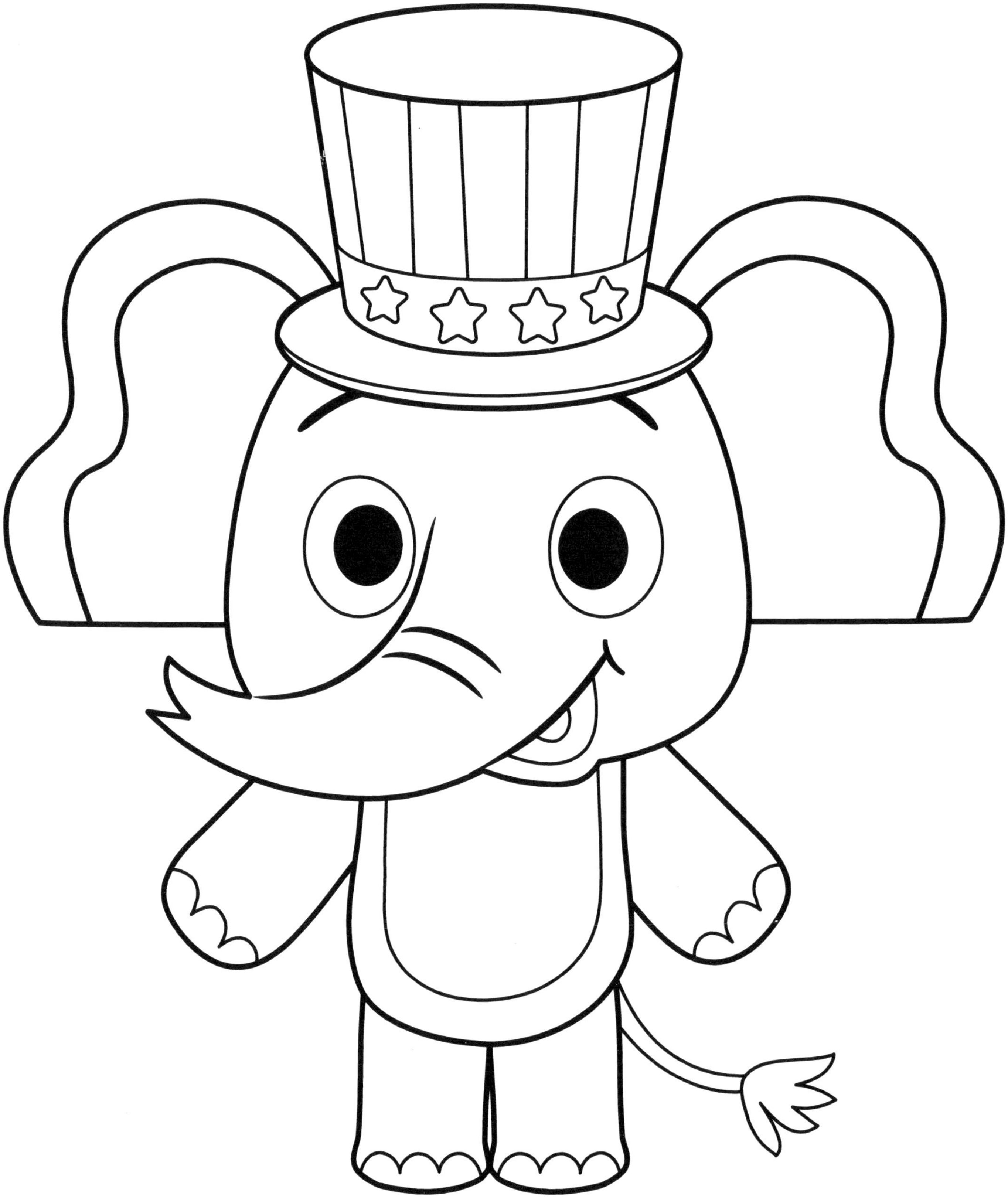